THE WORLD AROUND ME

WEATHER

IN MY WORLD

Written by

Hermione Redshaw

KidHaven PUBLISHING

Published in 2023 by **KidHaven Publishing,
an Imprint of Greenhaven Publishing, LLC**
2544 Clinton St., Buffalo, NY 14224

© 2022 Booklife Publishing
This edition is published by arrangement with
Booklife Publishing

Written by: Hermione Redshaw
Edited by: William Anthony
Illustrated by: Amy Li

Font (cover, page 1) courtesy of cuppuccino on
Shutterstock.com. With thanks to Getty Images,
Thinkstock Photo and iStockphoto.

Cataloging-in-Publication Data

Names: Redshaw, Hermione, author. | Li, Amy,
illustrator.
Title: Weather in my world / by Hermione Redshaw,
illustrated by Amy Li.
Description: New York : KidHaven Publishing, 2023.
| Series: The world around me
Identifiers: ISBN 9781534543423 (pbk.) |
ISBN 9781534543447 (library bound) |
ISBN 9781534543454 (ebook)
Subjects: LCSH: Weather--Juvenile literature.
Classification: LCC QC981.3 R394 2023 |
DDC 551.5--dc23

Manufactured in the United States of America

CPSIA compliance information: Batch #CWKH23
For further information contact Greenhaven Publishing LLC
at 1-844-317-7404.

Please visit our website, www.greenhavenpublishing.com.
For a free color catalog of all our high-quality books,
call toll free 1-844-317-7404 or fax 1-844-317-7405.

Find us on

Ben knows all about weather!
What will the weather be today?

It is **raining** outside.

Get your coat, Ben!

The ground is wet.
Ben splashes in puddles.

Ben's hair is getting wet.

Ben gets his umbrella.

There is a

rainbow

in the sky.

There is
a storm
outside!

Ben is staying inside today.

Ben sees a flash.

That was **lightning.**

Ben hears a BOOM.
That was thunder.

The sun
is shining.

It is warm
and bright.

Ben puts on his sunglasses.
Do not look at the sun, Ben!

Ben does not need
his coat today.

The ground is dry.

Ben has a picnic.

It is really windy.

Ben's umbrella is inside out!

Ben's hair is messy.

His cheeks are red.

The trees sway in the wind.

The wind whistles.

The wind is on Ben's face.

It is harder to walk.

It is snowing.

Ben loves the snow!

It is very
cold outside.

Ben needs his coat and boots.

Be careful, Ben!

The snow can be slippery.

Ben wears a hat, scarf, and gloves.

Ben's snowman wears them, too!

Ben's favorite weather is snow!

What is **your** favorite weather?